NTSB/MAR-09/02
PB2009-916402
Notation 7986A
Adopted April 7, 2009

I0413169

Marine Accident Report

Allision of Bahamas-Registered Tankship
M/T *Axel Spirit* with Ambrose Light
Entrance to New York Harbor
November 3, 2007

**National
Transportation
Safety Board**

490 L'Enfant Plaza, SW
Washington, DC 20594

National Transportation Safety Board. 2009. *Allision of Bahamas-Registered Tankship M/T* Axel Spirit *with Ambrose Light, Entrance to New York Harbor, November 3, 2007.* Marine Accident Report NTSB/MAR-09/02. Washington, DC.

Abstract: This report discusses the November 3, 2007, accident in which the tankship M/T *Axel Spirit* allided with Ambrose Light, an aid to navigation, at the entrance to New York Harbor. The impact left a 60-foot-long indentation and scrapes along the starboard side hull of the vessel and damaged Ambrose Light beyond repair. No injuries or pollution resulted from the accident.

The Safety Board's investigation identified the following safety issues: inadequate planning for the transit past Ambrose Light, inadequate bridge team communication during the approach to Ambrose Light, and failure to promptly report the allision and test for alcohol.

The National Transportation Safety Board is an independent Federal agency dedicated to promoting aviation, railroad, highway, marine, pipeline, and hazardous materials safety. Established in 1967, the agency is mandated by Congress through the Independent Safety Board Act of 1974 to investigate transportation accidents, determine the probable causes of the accidents, issue safety recommendations, study transportation safety issues, and evaluate the safety effectiveness of government agencies involved in transportation. The Safety Board makes public its actions and decisions through accident reports, safety studies, special investigation reports, safety recommendations, and statistical reviews.

Recent publications are available in their entirety on the Internet at <http://www.ntsb.gov>. Other information about available publications also may be obtained from the website or by contacting:

National Transportation Safety Board
Records Management Division, CIO-40
490 L'Enfant Plaza, SW
Washington, DC 20594
(800) 877-6799 or (202) 314-6551

Safety Board publications may be purchased, by individual copy or by subscription, from the National Technical Information Service. To purchase this publication, order report number PB2009-916402 from:

National Technical Information Service
5285 Port Royal Road
Springfield, Virginia 22161
(800) 553-6847 or (703) 605-6000

The Independent Safety Board Act, as codified at 49 U.S.C. Section 1154(b), precludes the admission into evidence or use of Board reports related to an incident or accident in a civil action for damages resulting from a matter mentioned in the report.

Contents

Figures

Acronyms and Abbreviations

AB	able seaman
ATON	aid to navigation
AIS	automatic identification system
ARPA	automatic radar plotting aid
BRM	bridge resource management
BTT	bridge team training
CFR	*Code of Federal Regulations*
DNV	Det Norske Veritas
ECDIS	electronic chart display and information system
GMDSS	global maritime distress and safety system
GPS	global positioning system
IMO	International Maritime Organization
Intertanko	International Association of Independent Tanker Operators
ISM Code	International Safety Management Code
NOAA	National Oceanic and Atmospheric Administration
RACON	RAdar beaCON
SOLAS	International Convention for the Safety of Life at Sea
SMS	safety management system
STCW	International Convention on Standards of Training, Certification and Watchkeeping for Seafarers
Teekay	Teekay Shipping Limited
TMS	Teekay Marine Services
TOTS	Tanker Officer Training Standards
VHF	very high frequency
VDR	voyage data recorder
VTS	vessel traffic service

Executive Summary

On November 3, 2007, about 0143 eastern daylight time,[1] the 819-foot-long Bahamas-registered tankship M/T *Axel Spirit* allided with Ambrose Light, an offshore aid to navigation located near the entrance to New York Harbor. The *Axel Spirit* was near the end of its voyage from Cayo Arcas, Mexico, to Perth Amboy, New Jersey, and was carrying 441,000 barrels of crude oil. The *Axel Spirit* sustained a 60-foot-long indent in the hull on its starboard side above the waterline and damage at the turn of the bilge. The vessel's hull was not punctured, no flooding occurred, and no cargo or fuel was lost. All three legs and the central column of Ambrose Light were damaged, causing the structure to lean. The tower's light beacon also stopped rotating at some point after the allision. Shortly after the accident, a Sandy Hook pilot boarded the *Axel Spirit* for the vessel's remaining transit to Perth Amboy. The pilot did not know that the *Axel Spirit* had struck Ambrose Light because he had not seen the damage to the vessel's hull, nor had the *Axel Spirit* bridge team informed him of the allision. The pilot also had not noticed anything irregular about the operation of Ambrose Light.

Damage to the *Axel Spirit* was estimated at $1.5 million. Ambrose Light was damaged beyond repair and was removed during the fall of 2008.

The National Transportation Safety Board determines that the probable cause of the allision of the *Axel Spirit* with Ambrose Light was the master's failure to use all available resources to determine the vessel's position and course in the transit past Ambrose Light and to adequately communicate his intentions and expectations to the bridge team, which therefore prevented the bridge team from appropriately supporting the master.

---

[1] All times in this report are eastern daylight time.

Factual Information

Background Information

Vessel Details

Vessel name	*Axel Spirit*
IMO No.	9282041
Owner/Operator	Axel Spirit, L.L.C./Teekay Shipping Limited (Teekay)
Flag	Bahamas
Type	Tankship
Built	2004, by Samsung Heavy Industries, South Korea
Classification society	Det Norske Veritas (DNV)
Construction	Steel
Length overall	819 feet (249.85 meters)
Beam	144 feet (43.79 meters)
Gross tonnage	62,929
Engine power and type	Slow-speed diesel
Service speed	15 knots
Horsepower	19,460 brake horsepower

Accident Details

Accident date	November 3, 2007
Time	0143 eastern daylight time
Location of incident	40 27′ N, 73 48′ W—Entrance to New York Harbor
Number of crewmembers	22
Injuries/fatalities	None
Damage	*Axel Spirit*, $1.5 million
	Ambrose Light, $10 million

M/T *Axel Spirit*

The *Axel Spirit* (figure 1), a 62,929 gross-ton motor tanker owned by Axel Spirit, L.L.C. and operated by Teekay, was built in 2004. The vessel was classified as an Aframax-class tanker.[2] Unlike very large and ultra large crude carriers that require wide channels and deep harbors, Aframax tankers can transit into most crude oil distribution ports. The *Axel Spirit* was double-hull, and tanks that were located next to its hull were void spaces or ballast tanks and did not hold any cargo or fuel oil.

---

[2] The term Aframax is derived from the average freight rate assessment tanker rate system. Aframax tankers range from 80,000 to 120,000 deadweight tons.

The *Axel Spirit*'s navigation equipment included two radars (10 and 3 centimeter) fitted with automatic radar plotting aids (ARPA),[3] an electronic chart display and information system (ECDIS), a global positioning system (GPS), and an automatic identification system (AIS). The vessel was also equipped with a very high frequency (VHF) radio, a global maritime distress and safety system (GMDSS), a speed log, a rudder position indicator, a rate of turn indicator, and an echo depth sounder. The *Axel Spirit* also had an onboard voyage data recorder (VDR) (see "Voyage Data Recorder" section for more information).

According to the crew and the Sandy Hook pilot, all of the vessel's navigational equipment was in good working order during the vessel's inbound transit to Perth Amboy. The equipment also functioned properly during the postaccident U.S. Coast Guard examination.

Figure 1. *Axel Spirit* near port. Photo provided by Teekay.

Teekay Shipping Limited

Teekay was formed in 1973. At the time of the accident, the company was one of the largest operators of medium-sized tankers in the world and had a fleet of 192 vessels of different types and sizes. Teekay's operational headquarters were located in Vancouver, Canada, and its

---

[3] A maritime radar with ARPA capability can create tracks of radar contacts. The system can calculate the tracked object's course, speed, and closest point of approach so that mariners can assess any risk of collision with another ship, an object, or a landmass.

corporate headquarters in Hamilton, Bermuda. In the summer of 2008, Teekay became the first shipping company in the world to be certified as voluntarily compliant with the Tanker Officer Training Standards (TOTS), a program established by Intertanko[4] earlier in 2008. The TOTS program was created to evaluate and ensure tanker officer competency across the industry by way of core competency-based training that, according to Intertanko, exceeds current minimum requirements. (For more information about Teekay, see section "Teekay General Procedures; Action Since the Allision.")

Ambrose Light

Ambrose Light (figure 2) was an aid to navigation (ATON) located in the approximate center of the heavily trafficked precautionary area[5] off the approach to the Port of New York/New Jersey (figure 3).

Figure 2. Ambrose Light before it was damaged. Photo by Asbury Park Press.

---

[4] Intertanko is the International Association of Independent Tanker Operators, established in 1970. Membership is open to independent tanker owners and operators; that is, non-oil companies and non-state-controlled tanker owners. About 80 percent of the world's tanker operators are independent, and most of them are members of Intertanko. Intertanko's mission is "safe transport, cleaner seas, and free competition." Intertanko has non-government observer status at the International Maritime Organization.

[5] A precautionary area is a transition zone where traffic intersects or transitions, such as near a pilot boarding area. Three major shipping lanes merge in the precautionary area off New York (the Nantucket to Ambrose Lane, the Hudson Canyon to Ambrose Lane, and the Barnegat to Ambrose Lane). Title 33 *Code of Federal Regulations* (CFR), 161.25, "Vessel Traffic Service New York Area."

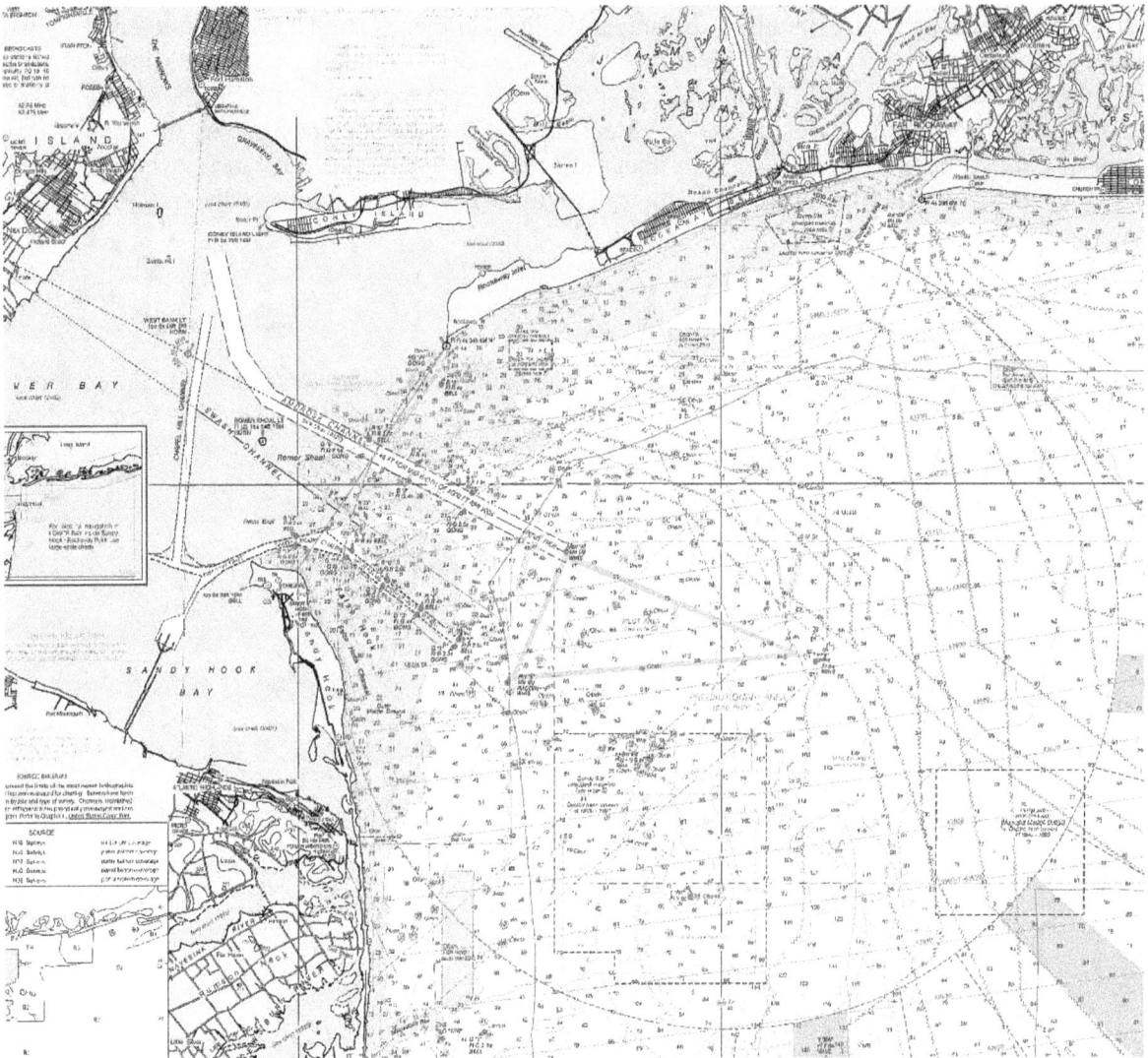

Figure 3. Section of National Oceanic and Atmospheric Administration (NOAA) navigation chart 12326, "Approaches to New York," showing the circular precautionary area with Ambrose Light near the center, the triangular pilot boarding area, the beginning of Ambrose and Sandy Hook channels to the northwest of the pilot boarding area, and part of the three traffic lanes (southern, southeastern, and eastern approach) leading to and from the precautionary area.

The tower, erected in 1999, was built on a pile system embedded into the sea floor and rose about 76 feet above the mean water level. Its rotating light sequence featured white light with a 60,000-candle intensity, flashing every 5 seconds. Ambrose Light was not protected by either a traffic separation zone,[6] which would restrict navigation within a specified distance of the structure, or by a physical barrier such as a fender system or protective pile structure. Since

---

[6] A traffic separation zone is a waterway management tool to establish an area or boundary inside which vessel navigation is prohibited. As an example, a 0.5-nautical-mile circular separation zone protects the lighted horn buoy located at the approach to San Francisco Bay, California. Separation zones help separate vessels traveling in opposing traffic lanes and around vital structures, such as light towers, to reduce the risk of collision or allision.

its 1999 installation, Ambrose Light had been struck by transiting vessels on two previous occasions, most notably in January 2001 by the 492-foot Maltese bulk freighter *Kouros V*, causing the tower more than $2 million in damage. A previous light tower in the area, originally erected in 1967, was also destroyed in a tanker allision, when the 754-foot Greek oil tanker *Aegeo* struck it in October 1996. The Safety Board did not investigate the *Kouros V* or *Aegeo* accidents.

Accident Narrative

The *Axel Spirit* departed the Petroleos Mexicanos marine oil complex at Cayo Arcas in the Bay of Campeche, Mexico, on October 27, 2007. The vessel was carrying 441,000 barrels of crude oil and was not loaded to full capacity (only to about two-thirds) so that draft restrictions could be accommodated at the discharge port. From Cayo Arcas, the *Axel Spirit* traveled northeast through the Gulf of Mexico, through the Straits of Florida, and north along the U.S. east coast. On November 2, the day before the accident, the vessel was on the last segment of its voyage to the Chevron facility in Perth Amboy, New Jersey. (For a detailed timeline of events on November 2 and 3, 2007, see appendix B.) Due to the *Axel Spirit*'s draft constraints at the intended berth, the vessel's arrival in Perth Amboy was planned around a local high water time with a mean saltwater draft of 34 feet. The original intent was to arrive near the high water time of 1444 on November 2; however, because of unfavorable seas in the latter part of the voyage, the vessel's estimated time of arrival in Perth Amboy was delayed from 1200 to 1700 on November 2. The next high water time was to occur at 0327 on November 3, and arrangements were made for a pilot[7] to meet the *Axel Spirit* about 0200 on November 3.

When the *Axel Spirit* arrived offshore in the early afternoon of November 2, the vessel proceeded to an anchorage about 4 nautical miles northeast of Ambrose Light to stand by for the 0200 pilot-boarding the following morning. The master chose the anchorage location in part because no telephone cables traversed the sea floor in that area; such cables could be damaged by or foul the anchor. At 1436 on November 2, the vessel was anchored and the master issued night orders instructing the watch officer on the bridge to monitor the radio and traffic, to observe the vessel's anchored position, and to call the master at 2350 for the shift into Perth Amboy.

About midnight on November 3, the master appeared on the bridge, where the second officer had the navigational watch. The crew began heaving anchor to prepare for getting under way toward the pilot boarding area. The third mate had tested the steering and navigation equipment during the 2000 to midnight watch, and it tested satisfactory. After the anchor was aweigh at 0042, the master tested the main engine ahead and astern, and the engine tested satisfactory. The master then put the engine to dead slow ahead (about 4.8 knots), and ordered the helmsman to come right to a course of 230. The master stated to the second officer that the 230 course appeared to be a good course to pass Ambrose Light, but he did not specify how far off the tower he wished to pass.[8] The master did not order the second officer to plot an intended

---

[7] A state-licensed pilot is compulsory for all vessels over 500 gross tons in foreign commerce operating into or out of the Port of New York/New Jersey. The pilot who boarded the *Axel Spirit* on November 3, 2007, was provided through the Sandy Hook Pilots Association, New York/New Jersey.

[8] Information obtained from the onboard VDR.

trackline for the *Axel Spirit*'s transit from the anchorage past Ambrose Light to the pilot boarding area, nor did the master plot any trackline on the chart himself. Teekay's safety management system (SMS) required that tracklines be plotted.

About 0115, after the vessel had gotten under way, an able seaman (AB) serving on the anchor detail reported to the bridge and assumed the duties of lookout. The bridge watch consisted of the master, the second officer, the lookout, and the helmsman. The master had the conn[9] and was controlling the engine from the bridge, giving course and rudder orders to the helmsman.

The master conned the vessel from a position near the center of the bridge (figure 4). The engine control was located just to the master's right. The vessel's ECDIS was located to the immediate right of the engine control. The vessel's 10-centimeter radar was located just to the right of the ECDIS, and the master told investigators that he could see on the radar the signaling of the RACON[10] on Ambrose Light. The master had an unobstructed view of Ambrose Light from his location on the bridge, and he told investigators that the visibility was good. He stated that, although lights on the shore at Sandy Hook were "confusing" and that they interfered with his observation of Ambrose Light, Ambrose Light itself "was a very sharp light."

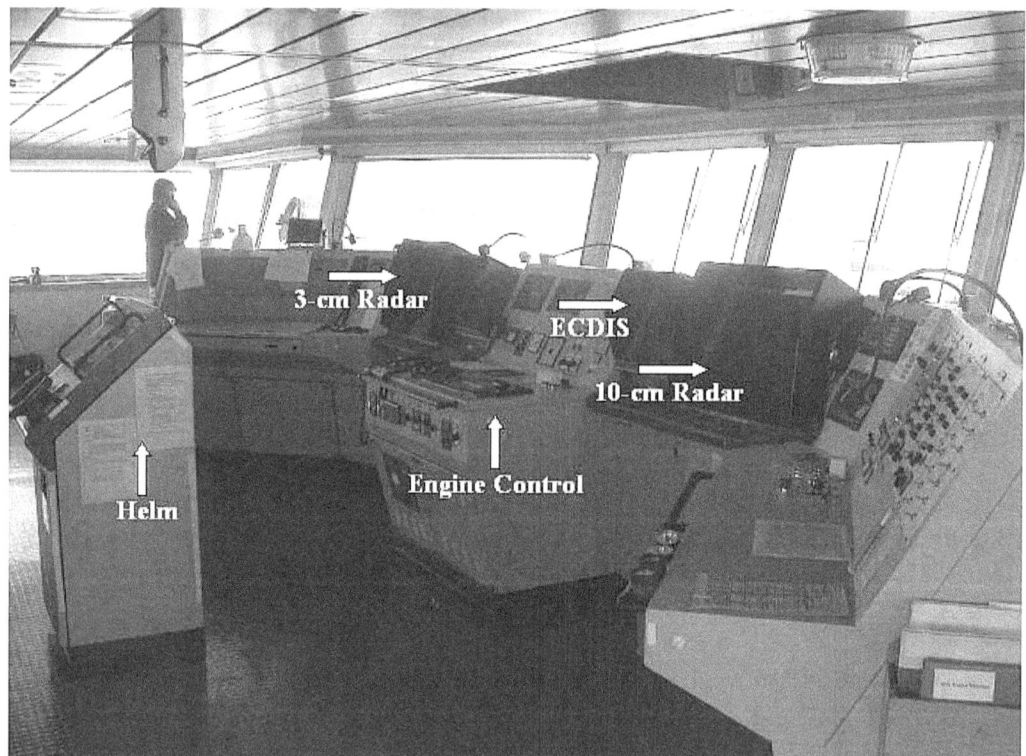

Figure 4. Layout of the navigation bridge on board the *Axel Spirit*.

---

[9] Navigational control of the vessel.

[10] RACON stands for RAdar beaCON and is a type of radar transponder commonly used to mark maritime navigational hazards. When a RACON receives a radar pulse, it responds with a signal on the same frequency, which leaves an image on the radar display. The image can help navigators identify navigation aids.

The pilot boarding area was about 4.5 nautical miles from the anchorage location. The *Axel Spirit* was ahead of schedule, causing the master to proceed at slow speed and to stop the engine on two occasions to consume time so that the vessel would arrive at the scheduled time of 0200. The first engine stop occurred at 0103 and lasted for about 11 minutes, until 0114. The second stop occurred at 0120 and lasted about 4 minutes, until 0124. The master told investigators that when he stopped, ocean swells caused the vessel to yaw 5 to 6 from the desired course.[11] At 0058, Ambrose Light was bearing 235 , about 3.5 nautical miles from the *Axel Spirit* (figure 5). The vessel's speed was 4 to 5 knots.

About 0112, the mate on the pilot boat *New York* called the *Axel Spirit* and asked the master which side of Ambrose Light he intended to pass to reach the pilot boarding area. The master responded that the *Axel Spirit* would pass south of Ambrose Light. The master told investigators that he had intended to alter course to a northwest heading after passing Ambrose Light for the remaining transit to the pilot boarding area. On being informed that the *Axel Spirit* would pass south of Ambrose Light, the mate on the *New York* informed the master that a pilot would board his vessel first and that the *Norwegian Spirit*, a large passenger ship still several nautical miles east of Ambrose Light, would receive a pilot second because the *Axel Spirit* was closer to the pilot boarding area.

The second officer used the 10-centimeter radar to take the bearings and ranges of Ambrose Light and plotted the position fixes on the navigation chart. At 0113, the second officer plotted the vessel's position on the chart, with Ambrose Light bearing 235 at a distance of 2.2 nautical miles. At 0118, the master remarked "too close" and ordered a slight course change to 225 to bring the vessel 5 to port. At 0122, the second officer recorded the vessel's position along the same bearing line of 235 , with the distance to Ambrose Light now 1.6 nautical miles. At 0134, with Ambrose Light still bearing 235 , the second officer recorded the vessel's position at 0.7 nautical miles from Ambrose Light.

In his interview with investigators, the second officer stated that he reported to the master the bearing and distance to Ambrose Light. However, in the VDR audio recording, the second officer cannot be heard communicating this information, nor did the VDR record the master asking for the vessel's bearing and distance to Ambrose Light. It did record him asking for the vessel's distance to the pilot boarding area. About 0119 on November 3, some 25 minutes before the allision, the VDR voice recorder captured the second officer telling the master that the pilot boarding area was 2.5 nautical miles away. About 7 minutes later, at 0126, the VDR recorded the master saying, "So... four miles and expected at two o'clock."

---

[11] To yaw is to rotate about a vertical axis. In navigation, yawing is brief deviation from the intended course.

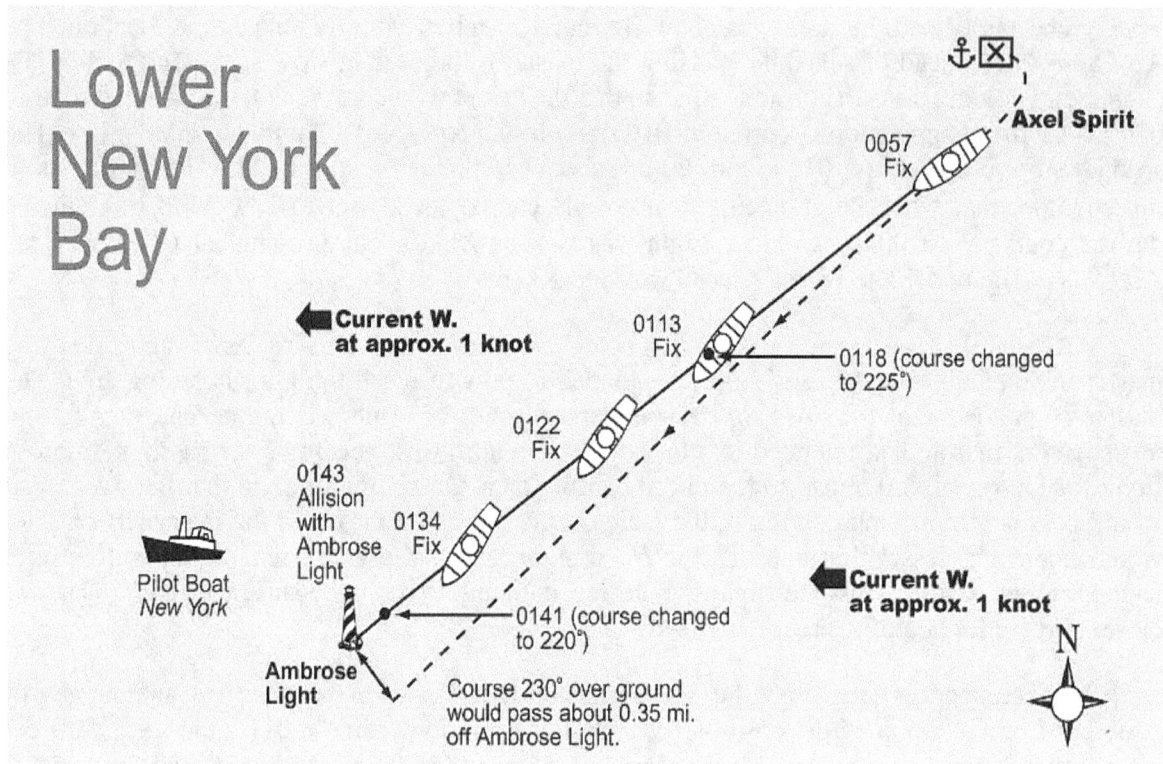

Figure 5. Graphic illustrating the *Axel Spirit*'s approach from the anchorage location toward the pilot boarding area. Image not to scale.

About 2 minutes before the allision, the bridge team was discussing the vessel's close proximity to Ambrose Light. Both the second officer and the lookout commented that the vessel was "very close" to the tower, and the master asked whether that meant "too close." The second officer responded yes. The master then ordered a course of 220 , another 5 to port.

Time[12]	Source	Communication
0141:21	Second Officer	Very close Ambrose Light
0141:24	Master	Huh?
0141:25	Second Officer	Ambrose Light is very close
0141:29	Master	Which one?
0141:30	Second Officer	This one this light on the starboard side
0141:33	Lookout	We are very close sir
0141:35	Master	Ambrose?
0141:35	Second Officer	Yeah

---

[12] The timestamp on the *Axel Spirit* VDR was determined to be minus 3 minutes 9 seconds from universal coordinated time (UTC). The time shown in this VDR transcript is eastern daylight time.

Time	Source	Communication
0141:37	Master	That one?
0141:38	Second Officer	That one
0141:40	Master	Too close you mean
0141:41	Second Officer	Yeah
0141:42	Master	So we can go two twenty [220]

Shortly thereafter, at 0142, the mate on the *New York* contacted the master via VHF radio to provide instructions as to the placement of the pilot ladder and boarding speed. This exchange lasted about 20 seconds. Shortly after the master finished the call with the pilot boat, the onboard VDR recorded the following:

Time	Source	Communication
0142:49	Helmsman	Two two zero sir
0143:01	Master	Come starboard ten
0143:03	Helmsman	Starboard ten
0143:03	Master	No port ten
0143:04	Helmsman	Port ten
0143:08		[Sound similar to engine telegraph]
0143:10	Helmsman	Port ten
0143:14		[Sound of impact]
0143:17		[Sound of impact]
0143:19	Master	[Expletive]
0143:23		[Sound of impact]
0143:23	Master	Starboard ten
0143:24	Helmsman	Starboard ten
0143:30		[Sound similar to engine telegraph]
0143:38	Helmsman	Starboard ten
0143:42	Master	Starboard twenty
0143:44	Helmsman	Starboard twenty
0143:53		[Sound similar to alarm tone]
0143:55	Helmsman	Starboard twenty sir
0143:56		[Sound similar to multiple alarm tones]
0144:06	Master	Hard a starboard
0144:07	Helmsman	Hard starboard

Time	Source	Communication
0144:08		[Sound similar to multiple alarm tones]
0144:23	Master	[Expletive] we touched

According to the VDR, the master gave a left rudder order, which he later explained to investigators was to maneuver the vessel away from Ambrose Light. When the tower was alongside amidships, the master gave a right rudder order, which he explained to investigators was to swing the stern away from the tower.

About 3 minutes after the impact, the VDR recorded the master stating, "my god this will be hell,"[13] and, "I wonder if it's showing much."

Sometime after the allision with Ambrose Light, the second officer entered in the *Axel Spirit*'s deck log of November 3, "0140 Vsl drifting near Ambrose LT, awaiting pilot. Due weather conditions & heavy sea vessel probably touched Ambrose LT."[14] The master told investigators that he did not perform any damage assessment of the vessel or direct the crew to do so because no alarms sounded, and the monitoring system showed no signs of water intrusion. Investigators later listened to the audio recording from the bridge, and a scraping noise followed by alarms could be heard on the recording.

In their interviews with investigators, each of the bridge team members described the encounter with the tower. Some felt a vibration and others stated that they saw a very bright light. The chief engineer, who was in the engineroom when the allision occurred, told investigators that he felt a sensation similar to that of a large swell hitting the hull but stated that that was a common occurrence offshore and that it did not seem anomalous to him.

About 0200, shortly after the *Axel Spirit* struck Ambrose Light, the Sandy Hook pilot boarded the vessel for the inbound transit through Sandy Hook Channel to Perth Amboy. The pilot boarded the vessel from the port side and did not notice the damage to the starboard side of the hull. About 0225, the pilot radioed the Coast Guard Vessel Traffic Service (VTS) New York to notify it that the *Axel Spirit* was about to enter the VTS New York coverage area, and, at 0226, the vessel proceeded into the VTS-controlled Sandy Hook Channel (see "VTS New York" section for more information). The inbound transit to Perth Amboy was uneventful, and, about 0600, the vessel was secured (portside to) at the Chevron facility's berth 1. The pilot departed the vessel at 0612. He later told investigators that he "had no complaints at all with the crew, captain, or the ship itself," and added that the *Axel Spirit* was a "very good handling ship" that performed well in the sea state. During the inbound transit, the master did not mention the allision with Ambrose Light to either the pilot or VTS New York.

For an hour and a half after the allision, no vessels reported seeing any damage to Ambrose Light, including the *Norwegian Spirit*, which was about 3 nautical miles east of the *Axel Spirit* when the allision occurred and passed Ambrose Light about 20 minutes later. At

---

[13] A separate Teekay submission has the master saying, "My god they drove me to hell."

[14] The vessel was under way, not stopped or drifting, from 0124 until about 0200 when the pilot boarded.

0315, the mate on board the pilot boat *New York*, which was still positioned in the precautionary area near Ambrose Light, noticed that the tower's rotating beacon was not functioning properly. The mate reported the discrepancy to VTS New York, which immediately issued a safety broadcast notice to mariners, urging caution while transiting the area.

In his interview with investigators, the mate on the *New York* stated that he was surprised to learn the following day that the *Axel Spirit* had allided with Ambrose Light. He confirmed that he had seen the vessel pass close to the tower—closer than other ships, which he said sometimes pass close as well. However, in his view, the *Axel Spirit*'s transit past Ambrose Light did not seem extraordinary based on what he saw on the radar, and he said that he had thought the vessel cleared the tower. It was not the role or the responsibility of the pilot boat and its crew to actively monitor or aid vessels transiting past Ambrose Light.

Later in the morning on November 3, after the *Axel Spirit* had been berthed for about 2 hours at the Chevron facility and after the vessel agent[15] had visited and departed the ship, the master personally observed the damage to the vessel's starboard-side shell plating, and alerted Teekay at 0813. About 0850, the master called the vessel agent's cell phone asking for assistance with reporting the allision to the Coast Guard. According to the vessel agent, the master stated that he had forgotten to tell the vessel agent while the agent was on board that morning that the *Axel Spirit* had "touched" the Ambrose Light platform on the way in. The vessel agent told investigators that he wanted to ensure that he correctly understood the master, and asked, "Do you mean you hit the platform?" According to the vessel agent, the master then responded yes. At the master's request, the vessel agent then notified VTS New York of the allision via telephone about 0852, which initiated the Coast Guard's sending an investigative team after more than 7 hours had elapsed since the accident. A representative from Teekay notified the Bahamas Maritime Authority of the incident via telephone on November 3 and followed up with a written report on November 4. The master submitted written notification to Teekay via e-mail on November 6 and attached the required Teekay SMS form.

Environmental Conditions

On the night of the allision, remnants of Hurricane Noel were passing offshore near the area.[16] The National Weather Service in Mount Holly, New Jersey, reported the winds at the time of the accident as 15 to 20 knots from the northeast, with gusts up to 30 knots, and sea swells between 5 and 8 feet in the area near Ambrose Light. The air temperature was 33 F. The *Axel Spirit* logbook listed the visibility at 12 nautical miles, winds between 12 and 27 knots from the northeast, and swells of about 6 feet from the northeast. The VDR on board the *Axel Spirit* indicated a wind speed of 15 knots, with gusts reaching 30 knots. The current near Ambrose Light, estimated at 1 knot, was to the west.

---

[15] A vessel agent handles business relayed from the charterer or owner of a vessel, such as arranging pilot and tugboat service, coordinating with port terminals for vessel arrival/departure, and handling matters related to U.S. Immigration and Customs Enforcement.

[16] At 0200 on November 3, 2007, the center of the disintegrating storm was located about 390 nautical miles south/southeast of Ambrose Light and was moving northeast away from the coast.

Damage

Axel Spirit. A damage assessment of the *Axel Spirit*, conducted at the Chevron berth on November 3, revealed damage to the vessel's starboard ballast tanks 4 and 5. Internal structural members (side longitudinals, transverse framing, and stiffeners) were buckled in the impact area (figure 6). Both tanks exhibited deformed side shell plating where the vessel allided with Ambrose Light. The hull plating was not penetrated but was inset above the waterline and at the turn of the bilge, running fore and aft about 60 feet, almost the entire length of each ballast tank (figure 7). The vessel's safety railing above the impact area was also damaged. The damage to the ship was estimated at $1.5 million.

Figure 6. Photo of damage to the interior hull, showing deformation and cracks in the starboard side longitudinals.

Figure 7. Photo of damage to the exterior starboard hull, showing buckled, scraped steel plates.

Ambrose Light. About 1300 on November 3, the pilot boat *New York* performed the first damage assessment of Ambrose Light. Subsequently, the Coast Guard assessed the damage. The tower had sustained damage to its three legs and to the center column, causing the structure to lean (figure 8). The southeast and southwest legs were inset, their welds partially or completely separated, about 8 feet above the waterline. The center column was distorted and the light beacon was stuck in one position, with the light on. The Coast Guard estimated that the tower was damaged beyond repair and would be removed. To construct another tower would have cost about $10 million.

Figure 8. Ambrose Light, leaning after sustaining damage. Photo by the Coast Guard.

Figure 9. Damage to Ambrose Light. Photo by the Coast Guard.

Incident Reporting

At the time of the accident, U.S. regulations for reporting a marine incident involving a foreign tankship operating in U.S. waters required vessel masters to immediately notify the nearest Coast Guard office after addressing any resultant safety concerns on board.[17] The vessel flag state of Bahamas required masters to make immediate notification to the Bahamas Maritime Authority, to be followed up as soon as practicable in written format. Teekay's SMS procedure regarding incident notification stated, "If in doubt, then notify," and required vessel masters to not only report to shore-side management all incidents meeting the company's criteria of a casualty, but to also report significant near-misses. (For more information about the SMS, see "Safety Management System" section.) According to this procedure, masters were required to initiate a series of notifications to minimize any adverse impact on the safety of the shipboard personnel, the vessel, the environment, and other waterway users. The master initiated notifications at 0813 on November 3 after he observed damage to the vessel's exterior hull at the Chevron facility.

Drug and Alcohol Policy and Testing

At the time of the accident, Federal requirements at 46 CFR 4.06 mandated that marine employers "take all practicable steps" to chemically test persons directly involved in serious marine incidents for evidence of drug and alcohol use. Alcohol testing was to be conducted within 2 hours of an incident and a drug test specimen within 32 hours of the incident, unless personnel was prevented from doing so by attending to safety concerns directly related to the incident. If more than 8 hours had elapsed since the incident, alcohol testing was not required. However, drug test specimens needed to be collected even if the 32-hour target window had passed.

Teekay also had a drug and alcohol policy in place, requiring unannounced drug and alcohol testing by a third party at least once a year on every vessel. In the event of a maritime incident or a serious personnel injury where alcohol or drugs could have been a factor, Teekay mandated testing. If shipboard staff conducted the test, pertinent information was required to be logged on an SMS form. This information would include date and time of the test, name and job position of person being tested, type of test performed, person administering the test, and the result of the test. Teekay's policy stated that masters were to ensure that drug and alcohol policies were enforced on board. Possession or use of illegal drugs was prohibited, but beer and wine were allowed within strictly defined guidelines. For example, alcohol consumption was prohibited in U.S. waters and during the 24 hours preceding arrival in port anywhere in the world. Any onboard alcohol use was subject to direct authority and control by the master. Teekay supplied investigators with a printout of sale transactions from the *Axel Spirit* bonded store, from which crewmembers could purchase beer and wine in limited quantities. According to the printout, which showed transactions for October and November 2007, the master had not purchased any alcohol from the vessel's store. The second officer was logged as having purchased one bottle of wine during the month of October; the exact date was not available.

---

[17] Title 46 CFR, 4.05-2(a), "Incidents involving foreign tank vessels," Part 4.05-20, "Report of accident to aid to navigation," and Part 4.05-1, "Notice of marine casualty."

The last unannounced, random third-party drug and alcohol test on board the *Axel Spirit* before the allision was February 8, 2007, while the vessel was docked in Venice, Italy. At that time, a representative from Marine Medical, Inc., boarded the *Axel Spirit* and collected specimens from all 22 crewmembers on board. The master on board the *Axel Spirit* in Venice was the same master as on the night of the allision with Ambrose Light. All of the specimens taken in Venice were later determined to be drug and alcohol free. The second officer, the lookout, and the helmsman on watch on the night of the allision with Ambrose Light were not on board the vessel in Venice and, therefore, were not tested that time.

About 0930 on November 3, 2007, 7 hours 47 minutes after the allision, the chief officer conducted the first recorded alcohol screening of the master, the second officer, the lookout, and the helmsman. The test was conducted using the onboard Draeger Alcotest tube, series CH 222, designed for initial alcohol screening. An annular ring was imprinted on the tube to mark blood alcohol content of 0.05. If exposed to alcohol in exhaled air, a yellow reagent inside the tube would change to green to indicate the presence of alcohol in the blood. According to the Draeger Alcotest tube instruction sheet, if the green discoloration reached the annular ring, blood alcohol content was 0.05 or higher. The CH 222 series test did not indicate specific levels above or below 0.05, only whether blood alcohol content reached 0.05. After conducting the test, the chief officer recorded the blood alcohol content for each crewmember as "0.0" on the Teekay form, at 0930.[18]

About 1900 on November 3, in accordance with Federal regulations, an independent drug testing service collected urine samples from the *Axel Spirit* bridge team. On November 6, all samples were reported as negative for the presence of amphetamines, cocaine, marijuana, opiates, and phencyclidine, the five illicit drugs tested for according to Federal regulations.

Master's Food-Related Illness

In his interview with investigators, the master said that about a week before the accident, he had returned to duty on board the *Axel Spirit* following a 4-month vacation. He said that shortly after returning on board, he contracted food poisoning, which he attributed to eating fish that the vessel's chief engineer had caught in Mexico. The chief engineer later confirmed to investigators that he had caught two tuna and brought them to the vessel's cook, who prepared both, ate one himself, and served the other to the master. The cook experienced no physical discomfort from eating the fish; only the master reported falling ill.

The master stated that he was ill with diarrhea and vomiting for about 4 days. The master told investigators that during his illness, he was able to regularly visit the bridge and conduct ship business but that frequent diarrhea and vomiting had disrupted his sleep, and he normally needed about 8 hours of sleep. The master told investigators that, at the time of the accident, he had been free from diarrhea and vomiting for 2 days, but still did not feel fully recovered, as his stomach was not yet completely normal and he still felt tired. The master stated that to treat the food poisoning he had ingested charcoal, which he obtained from the vessel's stock of medical supplies. Investigators examined paperwork from the *Axel Spirit*'s medical log and confirmed

---

[18] "Drug and Alcohol Testing Log (FM0063)," Version 2, dated November 3, 2007.

that "activated charcoal powder" was provided to the master on October 28, 2007. The master stated that in addition to the charcoal, he had added a high-fiber breakfast cereal to his diet, and he drank liquids to avoid dehydration. The master said that he did not choose to seek medical advice from shore during his illness.

The master told investigators that he had spoken on the telephone to a Teekay voyage manager during his illness and had told the voyage manager that he was sick. The voyage manager, who was based in Teekay's Glasgow, Scotland, field office, later confirmed to investigators that he had spoken to the master during that timeframe and that the master had mentioned to him having eaten fish that the master described to him as "dodgy." The voyage manager stated that the master had not indicated to him that he was ill with diarrhea and vomiting. The voyage manager told investigators that he had asked the master if he was all right, and the master had replied yes.

Before going on the bridge at midnight on November 3, the master had slept from 2130 until 2345. He told investigators that he considered himself fit to command the ship, and that he did not believe that his illness was a factor in the accident.

According to the second mate, the master looked and acted well while the vessel weighed anchor and proceeded into port. The lookout and helmsman agreed that the master seemed well. The mate on board the *New York* stated that the master's voice sounded clear and confident over the radio. The Sandy Hook pilot who came on board at 0200 told investigators that the master appeared well and competent and that they had a normal master/pilot conference.

Axel Spirit

Safety Management System

As required by the International Convention for the Safety of Life at Sea (SOLAS),[19] Teekay had an SMS that the company titled Marine Operations Management System. This system defined roles and responsibilities of all personnel, offered safe practices in ship operation and navigation, and established safeguards against all identified risks. As specifically required by the International Safety Management (ISM) Code[20] and as outlined in Teekay's SMS, it was the master's charge to implement the SMS on board, motivate the crew to observe the policy, verify that applicable requirements were adhered to, and review the SMS periodically for areas of improvement.[21] All of the officers on board the *Axel Spirit* had completed Teekay's SMS

---

[19] Chapter IX, Management for the Safe Operation of Ships, International Convention for Safety of Life at Sea (SOLAS) 1974, as amended, Regulation 3. SOLAS is the major international treaty addressing the safety of merchant ships. The first version of the treaty was adopted in 1914 in response to the sinking of RMS *Titanic*; there have been a number of amendments since.

[20] The ISM Code for the Safe Operation of Ships and for Pollution Prevention took effect in 1994, with the intent to ensure safety at sea, prevent human injury or loss of life, and minimize the risk of environmental or property damage. By 2002, almost all of the international shipping community was required to comply with the ISM Code, which, in part, meant having a working SMS.

[21] ISM Code and revised guidelines on implementation of the ISM Code by Administrations, 2002 Edition, 5.1, and Teekay Shipping Limited, Organization and Roles (OR0016), "Master Responsibilities and Authorities," Version 10.

training, including safety and environmental practices, operational orientation, bridge familiarization, and general review of responsibilities pertaining to their respective positions on board. On April 27, 2004, the ship's classification society[22] DNV issued a document of compliance to Teekay following DNV's satisfactory audit of Teekay's SMS. At the time of the *Axel Spirit* accident, Teekay's document of compliance was valid, and subsequent periodic verifications had been performed as required, with the most recent audit completed by DNV on April 31, 2007.

In addition, DNV had issued a safety management certificate to the *Axel Spirit* based on results of a shipboard SMS audit completed on November 3, 2004. The *Axel Spirit* had also passed an internal Teekay audit shortly before the accident on October 6, 2007. At the time of the allision, the *Axel Spirit*'s safety management certificate was valid, with an intermediate DNV verification performed December 19, 2006. A valid DNV-issued safety management certificate indicated that all of the vessel's key elements of the ISM Code were in place and satisfactorily implemented on board and that the master and officers were familiar with the company SMS. Federal regulations require both a valid safety management certificate and a copy of the company's valid document of compliance to be on board before vessel operation in U.S. waters. Both documents were carried on the *Axel Spirit*.

Teekay's SMS also required detailed berth-to-berth passage planning for all voyages. The second officer on the *Axel Spirit* had prepared such a passage plan on October 26, 2007, outlining the upcoming voyage from Mexico to New Jersey. The passage plan identified 33 waypoints for the *Axel Spirit*'s intended trackline and provided the bridge team with detailed navigational information for each waypoint. The information included the latitude and longitude of each waypoint, course to steer from each waypoint, distance of travel for each segment, remaining distance to go from each waypoint, underkeel clearance calculations, tide and current calculations, and minimum intervals for obtaining position fixes by sight, radar, and GPS. According to the passage plan and the paper navigational chart, the *Axel Spirit* was to proceed from waypoint 18 at sea to waypoint 19 in the pilot boarding area. At waypoint 19, the vessel would embark a local pilot and continue passing through the predetermined waypoints to the final destination at the Chevron facility. All members of the *Axel Spirit* navigation team had signed the written passage plan on October 26, and the master had approved it.

Because of the necessity to wait for the next high water time before arriving at the Chevron facility, the master diverted from the October 26 passage plan and navigated the vessel to the anchorage position northeast of Ambrose Light. According to Teekay's SMS, diversion from original and agreed-to waypoints required masters to revise or amend the passage plan. That requirement was also restated on the waypoint checklist in *Axel Spirit*'s passage plan. The checklist states in part, "Closely monitor execution of the passage plan and amend it if any waypoints are changed (e.g. vessel proceeding to anchorage instead of picking up pilot)." The second officer later told investigators that neither he nor the master revised the passage plan for

---

[22] In the shipping industry, classification societies are nongovernmental, independent, third-party organizations of ship surveyors that establish technical standards of design, construction, and survey (inspection) of ships and offshore structures.

the segment of the transit to the anchorage area or from the vessel's position at anchorage to the pilot boarding area before transiting those segments.

The second officer told investigators that, sometime on November 3, after the allision with Ambrose Light, he laid down a revised trackline on the paper chart for the segment from the anchorage position to the pilot boarding area (figure 10). He also generated an amended waypoint checklist, which he signed and inserted into the original passage plan. The second officer told investigators that no discussion about the original passage plan and navigational chart had taken place on the night of the accident because "there was no time to discuss" it.

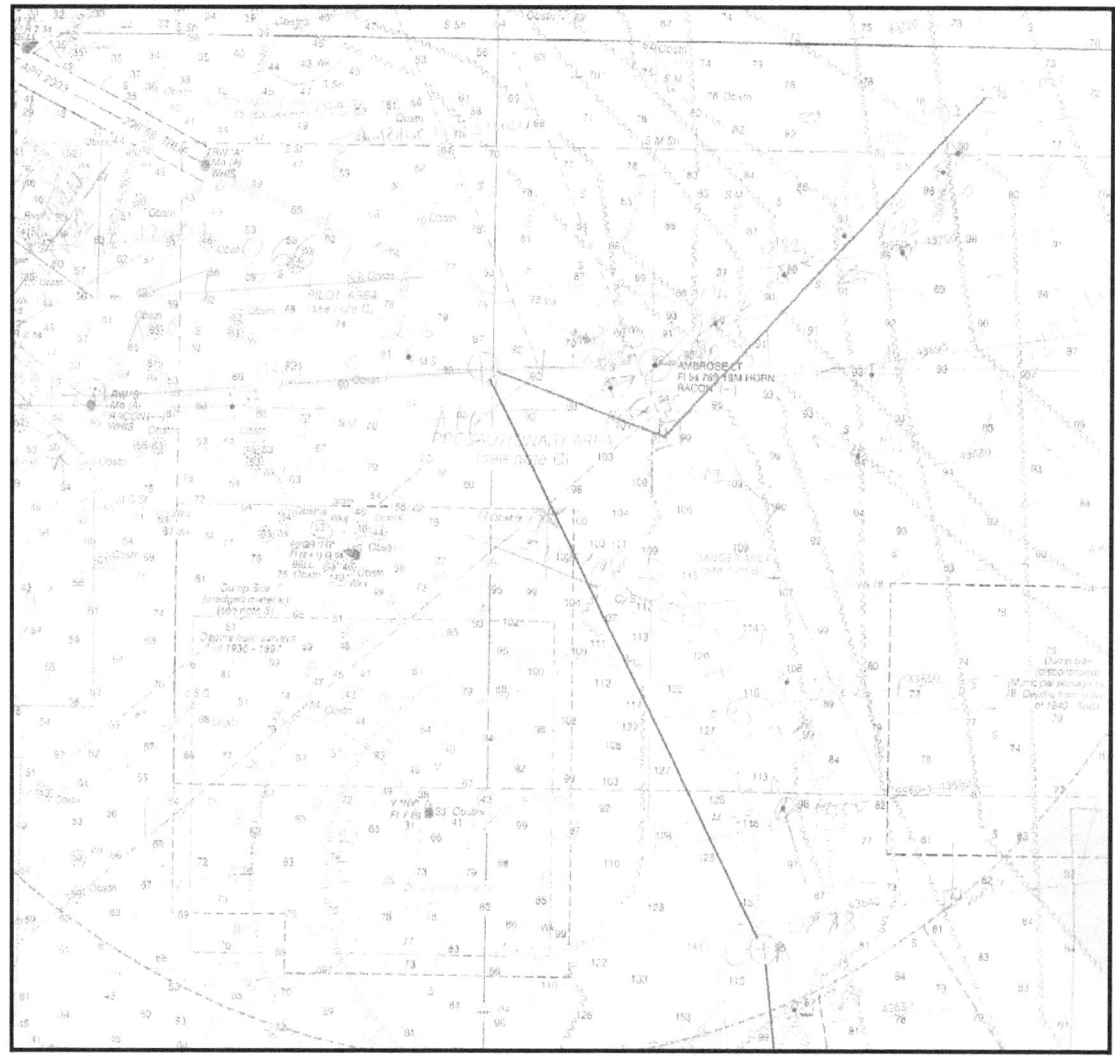

Figure 10. Extract from the *Axel Spirit*'s onboard navigation chart, with color enhancement added. The original intended trackline in the vessel's passage plan is overlaid in green, with waypoints 18 and 19 marked using small circles to intersect the trackline. The amended trackline that was placed on the chart by the second officer after the allision is overlaid in blue. Actual position fixes taken by the second officer on the 1200-to-1600 watch on November 2, 2007, and the 0000-to-0400 watch on November 3, 2007, are identified by a red dot. NOAA Chart 12326.

Teekay's SMS detailed what was expected of the bridge team to reduce the risk for error. The procedure reinforced the need for berth-to-berth passage planning. It also addressed the need for masters to adequately brief the bridge team before getting under way, communicate with the crew, use electronic navigation aids effectively, and maintain heightened awareness while on the bridge. Teekay's SMS regarding watch handover procedures at sea also required a clear announcement to the bridge team members as to who had navigational control of the vessel. The master told investigators that when he arrived on the bridge at midnight on November 3, 2007, he did not announce that he was taking navigational control. He told investigators that he felt the second officer must have assumed that the master had taken the conn, since the master was giving helm and engine orders.

Voyage Data Recorder

As required by SOLAS,[23] the *Axel Spirit* was fitted with a VDR. The VDR, a Samsung model, was tested and certified annually.[24] In addition to collecting data such as speed, rudder commands, and course, the VDR had a voice recorder, with microphones installed on the bridge. The VDR was designed to record about a 12-hour span of information and then continuously re-record and replace older data with newer data, unless and until the recording was preserved. Preserving the data entailed pushing and holding down a button for 5 seconds, which would save the previous 12 hours of data. All the available VDR information was analyzed during the course of this investigation.[25]

Teekay's SMS, in accordance with the International Maritime Organization's guidelines on preserving VDR data,[26] required vessel masters to ensure that VDR information was preserved as soon as possible following any significant incident or accident. However, about 1300 on November 3, when the Coast Guard boarding team arrived at the Chevron dock, the master had not preserved the VDR data, nor had anyone else among the *Axel Spirit* bridge team. Shortly after boarding the vessel, a member of the Coast Guard team pushed the VDR button and preserved the data.[27]

Personnel

Master. The master, age 60, started going to sea in 1963 as a member of the deck department on oceangoing ships on the Norwegian coast. After 3.5 years, he attended a

---

[23] Chapter V, Safety of Navigation, SOLAS 1974, as amended, Regulation 20.1.4.

[24] The last test before the allision was conducted in January 2007, when the VDR was certified operational as defined in the manufacturer specification. Compagnia Generale Telemar Limited, of Rome, Italy, issued the certificate of compliance on January 28, 2007.

[25] The VDR had not recorded the vessel's GPS information.

[26] Preservation of VDR data as specified in the International Maritime Organization's Marine Safety Committee Circular 1024, dated May 29, 2002, "Guidelines on Voyage Data Recorder (VDR) Ownership and Recovery."

[27] The preserved 12-hour VDR recording started about 0100 on November 3, some 45 minutes before the allision. Coast Guard boarding teams are required, according to the Coast Guard Marine Safety Manual, to ensure that VDR data is preserved as part of their vessel-boarding routine. The VDR preservation requirement is also addressed in the Coast Guard's training.

Norwegian navigation school and, after completing a 1-year course, acquired a mate's license. After he spent a few years as second mate, he was offered a temporary assignment as chief mate. He acquired a chief mate's license and continued to sail as chief mate. In 1982, he completed a master's course at a Norwegian navigation school and acquired a master's license. In 1993, he became master and served in that role thereafter. In 1999, Teekay bought the Norwegian company that the master worked for, and, after that, the master was employed by Teekay, including serving as master for 8 years on the *Kiowa Spirit*, an Aframax tanker like the *Axel Spirit*.

According to Teekay, the master had an excellent safety record and was well known and respected in the company. He had received high performance evaluations during his years of service and had no indicated deficiencies. In November 2004, a Teekay auditor assessed the master's performance while taking the *Kiowa Spirit* on an outbound transit through the Houston Ship Channel. The auditor found the master's performance "outstanding" and commended his "leadership and dedication to details."

In 2005, the master had renewed his Norwegian license. His last physical exam before the allision was on October 12, 2007, and he was found fit for duty. The master had taken all required courses in Standards of Training, Certification and Watchkeeping (STCW), including bridge resource management (BRM), and had taken a 5-day BRM refresher course in July 2006. He had served as master of the *Axel Spirit* for 5 months in the first half of 2007 and had then taken a 4-month vacation, returning to the ship about a week before the accident. The master stated that he was in good general health, wore reading glasses, and did not take any prescription medicine.

According to Teekay, the master had been nearing the end of a long mariner career when the accident occurred. Shortly thereafter, he voluntarily retired.

Second Officer. The second officer, age 42, stated that he had been going to sea for about 20 years. About 5 years before the allision with Ambrose Light, he had entered an apprentice program to become an officer. He stated that he acquired his first deck officer license in 2002 and that he had served as second officer on and off for about 2 years in periods ranging from 4 to 5 months, equating to about 16 months of service as second officer. The second officer's certificate of competency was issued by Poland and endorsed by the Bahamas. He was new to Teekay, having been first employed in June 2007. According to Teekay, the second officer scored well on testing in connection with applying for employment and had received a favorable first performance review by the previous master of the *Axel Spirit* in October 2007. The second officer had also taken the required STCW courses, including BRM. The second officer stated that he had been with the master for only about 2 weeks and felt that they had a good working relationship.

The second officer stated that he stood the 12-to-4 watches (that is, noon to 1600 and midnight to 0400). He usually slept from 0500 to 1100 and normally worked about 2 hours following the afternoon watch. When he felt the need, he occasionally took a 1- or 2-hour nap in the evening before going on watch at midnight. The second officer stated that he felt rested and well when he went on watch on the night of the accident.

Teekay had employed the second officer for less than half a year, and he was still under probationary employment at the time of the accident. Because of that and because Teekay considered his performance on the night of the allision unsatisfactory, Teekay dismissed the second officer shortly thereafter.

Lookout. The lookout, age 30, had been an AB on the *Axel Spirit* for about 4 months. He had been employed as an AB on various ships for about 9 years. He was a native of the Republic of the Philippines and had completed a 3-year course at the Maritime Academy in Cebu, Philippines, in 1997. The lookout completed a 1-year shipboard apprenticeship in 1998 and earned a license as officer in charge of a navigation watch issued by the Republic of the Philippines. His most recent license before the accident was issued on October 19, 2006.

Helmsman. The helmsman, age 41, had been an ordinary seaman on the *Axel Spirit* for about 4 months and had been employed by Teekay since 1992. He was a day worker under way and frequently served as helmsman. He was a native of the Republic of the Philippines.

Teekay General Procedures; Action Since the Allision

Teekay Hiring of Crew. In August 2008, investigators visited Teekay's operational headquarters in Vancouver, Canada, to learn more about the company's procedures with respect to safety, hiring and training of personnel, and oversight of fleet and crew. Management for the Teekay Marine Services (TMS) division, a subset within Teekay, told investigators that the company's evaluation and hiring of marine personnel was handled through its Glasgow field office, using a three-tier process. During the initial screening, applicants were reviewed for suitability, and their credentials were verified for authenticity by Teekay staff. In an effort to identify strengths and weaknesses of each candidate, applicants were also required to undergo a predictive assessment of their personality, conducted and evaluated by Teekay human resources staff. In the second tier of screening, applicants were asked questions that had been formulated based on the particular candidate's stated experience and level of license/credential held. Applicants seeking positions as either master or chief engineer would need to be vetted, accepted, and signed off by a Teekay executive holding a title of vice president or higher. In the third tier of screening, the candidates were further assessed during an orientation program, which acquainted the individuals with Teekay policies, expectations, and procedures, based on the applicants' respective positions. For senior-level hires, this orientation program was a 5-day process, conducted in the company's office and overseen by vessel managers. TMS management told investigators that Teekay also had its own seafarer's competency and performance program, which Teekay stated exceeded STCW requirements.

Teekay Internal Training Center. With respect to training its navigational watchstanders, Teekay had begun to establish its own training and development center before the accident and received the necessary flag state approval for the project in 2008. The training center is located in Glasgow and staffed by instructors and course-development personnel. The center also features a full navigation bridge and engine-control-room simulator. In 2008, Teekay appointed a chief instructor for bridge team training (BTT) and expected to deliver the first inhouse BTT and BRM training courses in April 2009. Teekay further expected to receive flag state approval for its BTT and BRM courses during the second quarter of 2009. The company also anticipated that its simulators, which were audited by DNV in late 2008, would receive DNV accreditation in the near future.

Teekay Oversight of Fleet and Crew. TMS management explained to investigators that oversight of fleet and crew was conducted using a "team" concept. The TMS division comprised multiple teams, each led by a fleet director, with each team responsible for the overall operation of 18 or 19 vessels. Within each team, the responsibility was subdivided into smaller groups consisting of voyage managers, purchasing agents, and vessel managers. Each of the subgroups managed the daily operation of three to four vessels, with the vessel manager holding the responsibility for crew performance and for the vessels' overall compliance with company policy and external regulatory requirements. TMS management told investigators that each fleet director held daily group meetings with subordinate personnel to discuss both the previous 24 hours of operation and the expectations for upcoming operations.

The *Axel Spirit* was one of several vessels in the team called "Lynx," managed by a fleet director in Glasgow. According to the Team Lynx fleet director, whom investigators interviewed from Glasgow by way of videoconference, the vessel manager for the *Axel Spirit* was required to make at least two random visits to the vessel each year. One visit needed to be a short ride-along trip to allow time for good communication and exchange between the vessel manager and the *Axel Spirit* crew and to allow for adequate underway assessment of vessel operations. The Team Lynx fleet director told investigators that in the months preceding the accident, the vessel manager had not been able to visit the vessel, due in large part to the *Axel Spirit*'s trade in the oil spot market.[28] The *Axel Spirit* and its crew had passed other recent audits, including the unannounced drug-and-alcohol test in Venice, Italy, in 2007, and Teekay's "Back to Basics" checkups, which entailed having experienced inspectors conduct periodic operational audits to assess bridge procedures employed on Teekay's vessels.

Teekay Internal Investigation. TMS management told investigators that after the company was notified of the allision with Ambrose Light, Teekay initiated its own internal investigation of the accident. It resulted in Teekay's issuing a fleetwide message from the president of TMS reminding navigational officers of their responsibility to exercise prudent BRM procedures and to report all incidents in a timely manner. In addition, TMS management told investigators that since the accident, the company had presented the facts about the allision to other mariners during scheduled meetings and workshops to encourage discussion and build on the lessons learned.

Revision to Teekay's Illness-Reporting Procedure. After the allision, Teekay modified its SMS shipboard procedure for reporting illness. The original SMS procedure had placed the illness-reporting responsibility solely on the master. The revised procedure now required the chief officer to share in the responsibility to notify the company. Teekay's intent in revising the policy was to double the likelihood that the company would be notified of onboard illnesses, especially those that might affect operational safety.

---

[28] The oil spot market is used in the oil industry to balance supply and demand. When a company temporarily has too much supply for its own needs, it will offer oil for sale on this market; likewise, if its oil supply is low, it will purchase oil on a shipment-by-shipment basis.

Coast Guard Action Since the Allision

Status of Ambrose Light

On November 5, 2007, the Coast Guard established a temporary safety zone within a 250-yard radius of the damaged Ambrose Light. In its announcement, 72 *Federal Register*, 65886, published November 26, 2007, the Coast Guard stated that the safety zone was needed because the malfunctioned tower was in danger of collapse and because surveying and debris removal was to take place. The temporary safety zone was to be in effect until May 5, 2008. On May 5, 2008, the Coast Guard extended the temporary safety zone until November 2, 2008, as published in 73 *Federal Register*, 30483, May 28, 2008. The Coast Guard stated that removing the ATON and associated debris would take about 75 days once started. The Coast Guard estimated that the removal would cost $850,000.

In the first months after the allision, it was unclear whether a new light tower would be constructed or whether current navigation technology, such as radar and GPS, made an ATON unnecessary in that location. On July 8, 2008, in correspondence to the Safety Board, the Coast Guard made clear its decision not to rebuild Ambrose Light after the damaged structure was demolished. According to the Coast Guard's correspondence, the decision not to rebuild was made in consultation with the New York and New Jersey pilots associations, including the Sandy Hook Pilots Association. Instead of rebuilding a tower, the Coast Guard would install floating light buoys. The tower was officially decommissioned in late July 2008, and, by October 2008, the last remnants of the tower had been removed.

VTS New York

At the time of the accident, the waters surrounding Ambrose Light were not included in VTS New York's coverage area.[29] The pilot boarding area and a significant portion of the precautionary area identified on NOAA Chart 12326 also fell outside the VTS New York coverage area. VTS New York did capture certain data on the *Axel Spirit*'s maneuvers near Ambrose Light, beginning about 0030 on November 3, 2007, which VTS computers later regenerated as part of the Coast Guard's accident reconstruction. The limited data included the vessel's course and speed, derived after the fact from VTS radar information and AIS data on the *Axel Spirit*.

Ports and Waterways Safety Assessment – New York

Between 1999 and 2001, the Coast Guard conducted a Ports and Waterways Safety Assessment of 28 ports around the United States. The Port of New York/New Jersey was not included in the assessment. In 2007, a group proposing to develop an offshore liquefied natural gas terminal conducted a study of the New York vessel traffic patterns and reported that over

---

[29] VTS New York actively monitors the entrance to New York Harbor and its two traffic channels, the Ambrose and Sandy Hook channels. VTS also actively monitors the area between the Verrazano-Narrows Bridge and the Throgs Neck Bridge in the East River, the area around the Holland Tunnel in the Hudson River, the Kill Van Kull strait and Newark Bay, and all of Arthur Kill strait and Raritan Bay.

4,900 vessels of greater than 10,000 gross tons traversed the precautionary area from November 2005 through October 2006.[30] This number did not include the many vessels of lesser tonnage transiting the precautionary area, such as leisure craft, fishing vessels, towing vessels, and commercial vessels under 10,000 gross tons. In June 2008, the Coast Guard announced that it would conduct a Ports and Waterways Safety Assessment of the Port of New York/New Jersey, starting in September 2008. The assessment would, in part, consider whether to extend the mandatory VTS coverage zone to include the entire precautionary area and whether to extend the approach channels to New York Harbor. After completion of the assessment in October 2008, the Coast Guard determined not to extend VTS New York's mandatory coverage zone. The Coast Guard extended the Ambrose approach channel and also moved the pilot boarding area eastward from its previous location. On being notified of the Coast Guard's decisions, NOAA published a revised chart on October 31, 2008, showing the new configuration (figure 11).

Figure 11. NOAA Chart 12326 "Approaches to New York," updated October 31, 2008, showing the extension of the Ambrose approach channel and the eastward relocation and reconfiguration of the pilot boarding area.

---

[30] Deepwater Port License Application, Atlantic Sea Island Group, L.L.C., Marine Vessel Traffic Patterns, Exhibit N, May 2007.

Analysis

Exclusions

Weather. Though the weather at the time of the allision was cloudy and blustery with wind gusts up to 30 knots, visibility was not restricted. The *Axel Spirit* logbook reported the visibility at 10 miles or more. The National Weather Service, Mount Holly, New Jersey, and the *Axel Spirit* logbook both reported sea swells ranging from 5 to 8 feet high. The current was about 1 knot to the west. Neither the sea state nor the current presented a significant hazard or unpredictability in navigating the medium-sized tanker. In addition, the Sandy Hook pilot was able to safely board the *Axel Spirit* in the prevailing sea state. The Safety Board therefore concludes that the weather conditions, though rough, were not causal in this accident.

Ambrose Light. By all accounts, Ambrose Light was functioning properly before the *Axel Spirit* allision. The master confirmed to investigators that, although in his opinion background lights on the shore melded with Ambrose Light and were somewhat "confusing," Ambrose Light stood out as "a very sharp light." The RACON on Ambrose Light also functioned properly. The master confirmed to investigators that he had seen the Ambrose RACON register on the *Axel Spirit*'s 10-centimeter radar during the transit from the anchorage location. The RACON's functionality was also confirmed when Safety Board investigators analyzed the VDR radar data. The Safety Board therefore concludes that background lights at the Highlands and Sandy Hook did not interfere with the ability to recognize Ambrose Light, which functioned properly before the allision and whose operation was not causal to the accident.

Functionality of the Vessel and Its Equipment. The *Axel Spirit* was equipped with modern navigational equipment, including radars, ECDIS, and AIS, that all worked satisfactorily according to the bridge team and the Sandy Hook pilot, and as tested by investigators following the accident, which included analyzing the *Axel Spirit*'s VDR data. The vessel's engine, propulsion, and steering also performed properly, as tested by the master and the third mate before leaving anchorage and as confirmed by the Sandy Hook pilot, who told investigators that the *Axel Spirit* was "a very good handling ship" during the transit into Perth Amboy. The Safety Board therefore concludes that the vessel's propulsion, steering system, and navigation equipment all functioned satisfactorily, and did not contribute to the accident.

Onboard Use of Illegal Drugs. The bridge team was drug-tested within the mandated 32-hour period, and all samples were reported negative for the five illegal drugs tested for. The Safety Board therefore concludes that drugs were not a factor in the accident.

Lack of Timely Alcohol Testing

The master's phone call to Teekay at 0813 on November 3, 2007, started the accident notification and chemical-testing process at a very late stage. At 0930, 7 hours 47 minutes after the allision, the chief officer tested the bridge team for alcohol and recorded the results as "0.0."

Though beer and wine consumption was permitted on board the *Axel Spirit* under strict guidelines, no evidence suggests that alcohol played a role in the accident. The Sandy Hook pilot who brought the *Axel Spirit* into port did not observe any behavior of the master or second officer consistent with impairment by alcohol. Neither did the Coast Guard boarding team that, nearly 11 hours after the accident, boarded the vessel about 1230. The Safety Board is, however, concerned that the alcohol testing was conducted too late to have any practical value. The human body metabolizes and eliminates alcohol at a rate of between 0.015 and 0.020 percent per hour. Because of the master's decision not to notify anyone of the incident until he had confirmed that the vessel had visible damage, the alcohol test was delayed until nearly 8 hours after the accident. The delay eliminated the chance to obtain meaningful results. The Safety Board therefore concludes that because alcohol testing was not conducted in a timely manner, no conclusive evidence exists as to whether alcohol played a role in the accident.

Failure to Follow All Aspects of Teekay's SMS

Investigators who examined Teekay's documents and interviewed company management concluded that Teekay was a well-organized shipping corporation with a good safety record. Teekay was also the first shipping company in the world to join Intertanko's TOTS program to enhance and ensure tanker officer training and competency. In addition, Teekay's SMS was comprehensive, and it clearly outlined company procedures and policies for risk mitigation; moreover, DNV had certified that Teekay's SMS met the requirements of the ISM Code and SOLAS. A month before the accident, Teekay had performed an SMS-related internal audit of the *Axel Spirit*. Safety Board investigators reviewed the paperwork associated with that audit and found it to be a thorough and systematic evaluation of both the vessel and crew. The scope of the audit was broad and the company auditor had examined in detail several areas of the ship and its functions, including the material condition, crew training and competencies, and the shipboard implementation of the company SMS. Overall, the audit findings were favorable and indicated that the SMS was in place, functional, and adhered to on board the *Axel Spirit*. After the *Axel Spirit* allision, Teekay took steps to reiterate to its navigational officers their responsibility to follow prudent BRM procedures and to report all incidents in a timely manner. Teekay also broadened its illness-reporting policy, placing the responsibility to report onboard illnesses not just on masters, but on chief officers as well. Finally, as a result of the accident, Teekay ended its relationship with the master and the second officer. The Safety Board concludes that Teekay's operational oversight and commitment to safety were adequate.

Despite Teekay's organization and thorough SMS policies, the master did not follow certain aspects of the SMS on the night of the allision, and he did not require the navigational crew to comply with critical risk-mitigation procedures. The master told investigators that to enforce the SMS was paperwork-intensive and difficult, and he felt that the system was "huge." Because the master felt that the SMS was overwhelming, he was disinclined to follow certain procedures in it. This was evident in several areas, as explained below.

Teekay's SMS required that bridge teams communicate effectively, act in close coordination with others on watch, and use all available resources to detect risk of collision with other vessels or allision with fixed objects. For example, one of the available onboard tools for risk mitigation was the ARPA feature on the vessel's radars. If the ARPA had been used to track

Ambrose Light, it would have calculated the tower's closest point of approach and the time at which the ship would pass it. The master and the second officer were both familiar with using ARPA, yet investigators found no evidence that the ARPA was used to track Ambrose Light on the night of the accident, or that the *Axel Spirit* bridge team had communicated about using it. The Safety Board therefore concludes that the master had first-rate navigation equipment, an experienced navigational officer, and a lookout on the bridge, yet failed to use these resources effectively.

Leading up to the allision, communication among the bridge team, especially between the master and the second officer, was limited. When the master arrived on the bridge at midnight on November 2, the second officer was the scheduled navigational watch officer for the 0000-to-0400 watch. The master took the conn without announcing to the bridge team that he was doing so. He confirmed to investigators that he had not made an announcement to the second officer, but told investigators that he felt the second officer must have assumed that the master had formally taken the conn since the master was giving helm and engine orders. At any rate, the VDR did not indicate that a bridge team briefing of any kind took place as the vessel got under way toward the pilot boarding area. Moreover, the VDR indicated that the master may not have correctly interpreted some of the information he was given. About 0119, the second officer informed the master that the distance from the *Axel Spirit* to the pilot boarding area was 2.5 nautical miles. However, about 7 minutes later, the VDR recorded the master saying, "So... four miles and be expected at two o'clock." No one on the bridge was heard correcting the master for his failure to account for the forward progress of the vessel. Nor was anyone heard pointing out that 7 minutes earlier, the second officer had informed the master that the pilot boarding area was 2.5 nautical miles away, not 4. The master seemed to have lost awareness of the vessel's position, and he navigated as if the pilot boarding area and Ambrose Light were 1.5 nautical miles farther away than they were.

From 0113 to 0134, the second officer plotted three positions of the ship relative to Ambrose Light, each with a constant bearing of 235 and decreasing range. As the *Axel Spirit* approached Ambrose Light, the 235 bearing should have opened on the starboard bow—that is, changed to the right. The fact that it did not should have alerted the bridge team, particularly the second officer, that the *Axel Spirit* was on a collision course with the tower. Yet the vessel's VDR does not indicate that the second officer ever relayed the critical navigation information to the master, nor did the master specifically ask for the bearing to Ambrose Light or the vessel's distance from it. The Safety Board therefore concludes that the communication between the master and the second officer was limited and ineffective, culminating in a failure to process and share critical navigation information about the vessel's precarious situation.

Teekay's SMS also required thorough, continuous passage planning. The *Axel Spirit*'s original passage plan of October 26, 2007, which covered the voyage from Cayo Arcas, Mexico, to Perth Amboy, New Jersey, was detailed and successfully executed by the bridge team until the vessel diverted to anchorage in New York Harbor to await the next high water time. According to Teekay's SMS, the master was responsible for ensuring that passage plan procedures were followed, and the second officer was responsible for updating the passage plan once the vessel diverted to anchorage. On the afternoon of November 2, the master did some planning for anchoring the vessel, selecting a location where no telephone cables traversed the sea floor, but he did not amend the passage plan. And when the master arrived on the bridge at midnight on

November 3 to prepare for getting under way to the pilot boarding area, he initiated no amendments to the passage plan.

The nearly 10 hours at anchorage on November 2 would have provided a good opportunity to revise the passage plan. During this time, the master could have consulted with the second officer about the intended transit to the pilot boarding area, including determining a safe distance from Ambrose Light that the vessel should maintain. A conference between the master and the second officer could also have ensured that both individuals understood precisely what was expected during the transit past Ambrose Light, and it may have enabled a more effective exchange of information relative to the master's navigational intentions. Also while at anchorage, an appropriate trackline past Ambrose Light should have been plotted, but this important navigation task was not performed. The trackline could have been used as a navigational tool to monitor the progress of the vessel—if the ship drifted off the trackline, the second officer could have made a specific report as to how far off-course the vessel was, which way the vessel was setting, and how to compensate for the current. A trackline could also have facilitated the optional use of parallel indexing[31] to guide the vessel as it proceeded toward Ambrose Light. If the master had required a plotted trackline from the anchorage location to the pilot boarding area and had clearly communicated his intentions to the bridge team, deviations from that plan and trackline could have alerted the team that the vessel was off-course. However, no trackline from the anchorage location to the pilot boarding area was plotted before the *Axel Spirit* started that segment. Instead, the master navigated by seaman's eye. The Safety Board therefore concludes that amending the passage plan as required by Teekay's SMS, plotting a trackline before making the transit from anchorage to the pilot boarding area, and then following that trackline during the transit could have prevented the allision with Ambrose Light.

The master also did not sufficiently account for the current to the west during the transit toward the pilot boarding area. When the vessel left the anchorage location, the master chose to steer a 230 course. At that time, Ambrose Light was bearing 235, so 230 appeared a reasonable starting course. However, the *Axel Spirit* departed the anchorage location too early for a 4.5-nautical-mile transit to the pilot boarding area, and the intermittent stopping of the engine and proceeding at dead slow to consume time allowed the current to carry the light-loaded vessel farther west and onto a path with the tower. In addition, during the hour of transit from the anchorage location to Ambrose Light, the *Axel Spirit* gradually moved to the right of the master's intended track, which the master seemed to realize about 0118 when he remarked "too close" and ordered the course adjusted to 225. But this minor 5 course change, followed about 0141 by another 5 change to 220, was not enough to correct the situation. At that point, the vessel needed to make a course change three to five times greater to clear Ambrose Light than what the master ordered. The Safety Board therefore concludes that during the transit from the anchorage location to the pilot boarding area, the master did not focus his attention on safely navigating around Ambrose Light and failed to compensate for the current's effect on the vessel's set and drift toward Ambrose Light.

---

[31] Parallel indexing is a navigational technique that involves creating on the radar screen a line that is parallel to the ship's course, but offset to the left or right by some distance. This parallel line allows the navigator to maintain a given distance from hazards.

Master's Alertness and Physical Condition

During the transit from the anchorage location to the pilot boarding area, the master seemed confused about targets on the 10-centimeter radar. As captured by the VDR, his uncertainty seemed particularly evident at 0141, about 2 minutes before the allision. When the second officer and the lookout both reported the vessel's close proximity to Ambrose Light, the master asked the second officer for clarification of targets displayed on the radar and for the second officer to point out the tower to him. The second officer was also heard having to repeat information for the master to hear or understand it. Further, the master did not seem to comprehend the developing urgency to steer the vessel away from Ambrose Light. Less than 2 minutes before the allision, and with Ambrose Light straight ahead and clearly in sight, the master ordered the helmsman to steer 220 , only 5 to port from the 225 course the vessel had been maintaining. Within a minute and a half of the master's 220 helm order, the helmsman confirmed the vessel's course as 220 . The master then incorrectly ordered the helmsman to input 10 starboard rudder, but quickly corrected the order to 10 port rudder, which was still too minor a course adjustment and came too late to avoid the allision.

The master's alertness may have been degraded because of his physical condition on the night of the accident. The master told investigators that in the week leading up to the allision, he had suffered from diarrhea and vomiting for about 4 days, and that the illness had been severe enough to disrupt his sleep. However, the master said that he had been free from diarrhea and vomiting for about 2 days before the accident, and that he had taken a 2-hour nap before getting under way from the anchorage location. He told investigators that he had felt well enough to have the conn. Nevertheless, the master's ongoing recovery may have affected his alertness. The Safety Board therefore concludes that the master's physical condition on the night of the accident may have caused his loss of situational awareness with regard to the vessel's position and cannot be excluded as a factor in the accident.

Lack of Timely Accident Notification

The master did not promptly notify the Coast Guard, Teekay, or the Bahamas Maritime Authority of his vessel's allision with Ambrose Light. Furthermore, the pilot who boarded the vessel after the allision was not informed of the accident. The master also did not take action to preserve the onboard VDR data, nor did any other member of the *Axel Spirit* bridge team. The VDR information was not preserved until nearly 11 hours after the accident, when a member of the Coast Guard boarding team secured the data. Because of the delay, pertinent accident data were nearly lost, as the preserved recording started about 0100 on November 3, only some 45 minutes before the accident. The Safety Board therefore concludes that only by the prompt action of the Coast Guard boarding team was the vessel's critical VDR data of the accident preserved.

In addition, the master did not conduct a prompt damage assessment of the vessel, despite the fact that in the VDR audio recording, the impact of the vessel's hull with Ambrose Light is heard clearly. The master told investigators that no alarms sounded after the allision, but in the VDR audio recording, multiple alarms are heard sounding on the bridge within seconds of the impact. The VDR also captured the master expressing concern about the potential harsh reaction to the incident, wondering whether the damage to the vessel was obvious, stating, "[expletive] we touched," and "I wonder if it's showing much." Given the sound of the impact, the sound of alarms that followed, and the master's verbal reaction, it seems clear that the master realized fully that the vessel had allided with Ambrose Light. As a result of the allision, the vessel could have sustained flooding, structural damage, or release of cargo. Yet no shipboard announcement was made, no general alarm was sounded, and no thorough damage assessment was conducted on board following the allision. Instead, the master relied solely on tank remote monitoring alarms. The Safety Board therefore concludes that the master's failure to adequately assess the damage to the vessel could have placed the vessel, its crew, and the environment at risk.

The master also did not take the time to ascertain whether Ambrose Light had been damaged, and instead continued the vessel's transit to the pilot boarding area after alliding with the tower. Not until more than 7 hours after the allision, and only after confirmation of visible damage to the hull, did the master start the notification process. However, it was the mate on the pilot boat *New York* who, about an hour and a half after the allision, noticed and promptly alerted VTS New York that Ambrose Light had malfunctioned. Many vessels, especially smaller ones without high-technology equipment on board, depended on Ambrose Light for navigation guidance. Because the allision left the tower's rotating light stuck in one fixed position, some mariners approaching the precautionary area would not have been able to see Ambrose Light, depending on the direction from which they were approaching, and might not have known anything was amiss with the light. The Safety Board therefore concludes that the master's failure to notify authorities of the allision with Ambrose Light placed other mariners using the waterway at risk.

The mate on the pilot boat *New York* was not responsible for monitoring the functionality of Ambrose Light, but nevertheless noticed that the tower's light beacon had stopped rotating. On making that observation, the mate notified VTS New York, which in turn alerted mariners. The Safety Board therefore concludes that the mate on the pilot boat took appropriate action to reduce risk to mariners by promptly notifying VTS New York that Ambrose Light had malfunctioned.

Conclusions

Findings

1. The weather conditions, though rough, were not causal in this accident.

2. Background lights at the Highlands and Sandy Hook did not interfere with the ability to recognize Ambrose Light, which functioned properly before the allision and whose operation was not causal to the accident.

3. The vessel's propulsion, steering system, and navigation equipment all functioned satisfactory, and did not contribute to the accident.

4. Drugs were not a factor in the accident.

5. Because alcohol testing was not conducted in a timely manner, no conclusive evidence exists as to whether alcohol played a role in the accident.

6. Teekay's operational oversight and commitment to safety were adequate.

7. The master had first-rate navigation equipment, an experienced navigational officer, and a lookout on the bridge, yet failed to use these resources effectively.

8. The communication between the master and the second officer was limited and ineffective, culminating in a failure to process and share critical navigation information about the vessel's precarious situation.

9. Amending the passage plan as required by Teekay's safety management system, plotting a trackline before making the transit from anchorage to the pilot boarding area, and then following that trackline during the transit could have prevented the allision with Ambrose Light.

10. During the transit from the anchorage location to the pilot boarding area, the master did not focus his attention on safely navigating around Ambrose Light and failed to compensate for the current's effect on the vessel's set and drift toward Ambrose Light.

11. The master's physical condition on the night of the accident may have caused his loss of situational awareness with regard to the vessel's position and cannot be excluded as a factor in the accident.

12. Only by the prompt action of the Coast Guard boarding team was the vessel's critical VDR data of the accident preserved.

13. The master's failure to adequately assess the damage to the vessel could have placed the vessel, its crew, and the environment at risk.

14. The master's failure to notify authorities of the allision with Ambrose Light placed other mariners using the waterway at risk.

15. The mate on the pilot boat took appropriate action to reduce risk to mariners by promptly notifying VTS that Ambrose Light had malfunctioned.

Probable Cause

The National Transportation Safety Board determines that the probable cause of the allision of the *Axel Spirit* with Ambrose Light was the master's failure to use all available resources to determine the vessel's position and course in the transit past Ambrose Light and to adequately communicate his intentions and expectations to the bridge team, which therefore prevented the bridge team from appropriately supporting the master.

BY THE NATIONAL TRANSPORTATION SAFETY BOARD

MARK V. ROSENKER
Acting Chairman

ROBERT L. SUMWALT
Member

DEBORAH A. P. HERSMAN
Member

STEVEN R. CHEALANDER
Member

KATHRYN O'LEARY HIGGINS
Member

Adopted: April 7, 2009

Appendixes

Appendix A

Investigation

The Safety Board was notified of the *Axel Spirit* accident by Coast Guard headquarters about 1000 on November 4, 2007, about 32 hours after the accident, and launched a team of three investigators to New York at 1400. The launch team consisted of an investigator-in-charge, a deck operations investigator, and an investigator specializing in Coast Guard vessel traffic service and accident notification procedures. During the on-scene investigation, the team was augmented by staff from the Safety Board's research and engineering division, who retrieved data from the vessel's VDR and ECDIS.

The Safety Board investigated the accident under the authority of the Independent Safety Board Act of 1974, according to the Board's rules. The parties to the investigation were the U.S. Coast Guard, Teekay, and the Sandy Hook Pilots Association.

Appendix B

Detailed Timeline

November 2, 2007

0942   The Coast Guard set hurricane condition II for all units in the area of responsibility, including Sector New York, anticipating remnants from Hurricane Noel to pass through the area.

1044   Sector New York set hurricane condition Yankee[32] for the Port of New York/New Jersey.

1436   *Axel Spirit* anchored 3.9 nautical miles from Ambrose Light at position 40 29′ N 073 44′ W.

1920   The Coast Guard set hurricane condition I for all Coast Guard units and assets in the area of responsibility, including Sector New York.

2018   Sector New York set hurricane condition Zulu[33] for the Port of New York/New Jersey in the anticipation of potential gale forces winds along the coast within the next 12-hour period.

November 3, 2007

0000   Master arrived on the bridge of the *Axel Spirit*.

0015   Master ordered crew to begin heaving anchor.

0042   Anchor was aweigh and the *Axel Spirit* began shift from the anchorage location toward the pilot boarding area.

0143   *Axel Spirit* allided with Ambrose Light.

0200   *Axel Spirit* arrived at pilot boarding area and a Sandy Hook pilot came on board.

0225   Sandy Hook pilot provided VTS New York with *Axel Spirit*'s sailing plan.

0226   *Axel Spirit* entered VTS-controlled waters.

---

[32] Hurricane condition Yankee is set when gale force winds (34 knots) are expected within 24 hours.

[33] Hurricane condition Zulu is set when gale force winds (34 knots) are expected within 12 hours.

0315	VTS received communication from the Sandy Hook pilot vessel *New York* that Ambrose Light was not functioning properly. VTS logged an ATON Discrepancy Report and began sending a broadcast notice to mariners via VHF.
0410	Docking pilot boarded the *Axel Spirit*.
0454	First line passed from the vessel to the Chevron facility at Perth Amboy.
0600	*Axel Spirit* secured at the Chevron facility.
0606	*Axel Spirit* finished with engines.
0612	Gangway in place and both pilots disembarked the vessel.
0618	Vessel agent boarded the *Axel Spirit*.
0630	Vessel commenced transfer of cargo to facility ashore.
0642	Vessel agent disembarked the *Axel Spirit*.
0813	Master reported the allision to Teekay's "First Alert" center.
0850	Master contacted vessel agent to request assistance in notifying the Coast Guard of the allision.
0852	VTS received communication from the vessel agent, stating that the master informed the agent that the *Axel Spirit* may have allided with Ambrose Light. Sector New York began notification procedures detailed in Quick Response Card (QRC) VTS-6, Vessel Grounding or Collisions.
0905	Sector New York investigators/response team notified and dispatched.
1130	Sector New York requested assistance from pilot vessel *New York* in assessing damage to Ambrose Light.
1230	Sector New York investigators/response team arrived on *Axel Spirit*.
1257	Pilot vessel *New York* reported to Sector New York that Ambrose Light had significant damage.
1300	Sector New York investigator pushed and held down the button on the vessel's VDR to preserve critical voyage information.
1343	VTS began broadcast of safety marine information bulletin via VHF radio informing mariners of the ATON discrepancy.
1800	The Coast Guard stood down units from Hurricane Condition I status.

November 4, 2007

0334 Coast Guard headquarters notified the NTSB communication center via e-mail of the vessel allision and the condition of Ambrose Light.

0927 A representative from the Coast Guard Ocean Engineering Division copied the Safety Board communication center on an e-mail, expanding on contents of earlier Coast Guard e-mail relating to the allision.

0932 NTSB communication center forwarded Coast Guard e-mail string to Deputy Director, Office of Marine Safety and MS duty officer.

1104 Duty officer forwarded Coast Guard e-mail string to Deputy Director and Director, Office of Marine Safety.

1137 Deputy Director, Office of Marine Safety, contacted senior marine investigation staff by telephone, forwarded e-mail notification to same, and initiated launch of Go Team.

1218 Sector New York submitted written synopsis of casualty to Coast Guard headquarters.